An Introduction to Improving
Your Self-esteem

2nd Edition

Melanie Fennell with Lee Brosan

ROBINSON

ROBINSON

First published in Great Britain in 2020 by Robinson

1 3 5 7 9 10 8 6 4 2

Copyright © Melanie Fennell and Lee Brosan, 2020

The moral right of the authors has been asserted.

Important note
This book is not intended as a substitute for medical advice or
treatment. Any person with a condition requiring medical attention
should consult a qualified medical practitioner or suitable therapist.

A CIP catalogue record for this book
is available from the British Library.

ISBN: 978-1-47214-018-0

Typeset in Bembo by Initial Typesetting Services, Edinburgh
Printed and bound in Great Britain by Clays Ltd, Elcograf S.p.A.

Papers used by Robinson are from well-managed forests and
other responsible sources.

MIX
Paper from
responsible sources
FSC® C104740

Robinson
An imprint of
Little, Brown Book Group
Carmelite House
50 Victoria Embankment
London EC4Y 0DZ

An Hachette UK Company
www.hachette.co.uk

www.littlebrown.co.uk

Contents

About This Book   vii

Part 1: Understanding Low Self-esteem   1

1 What Is Low Self-esteem?   3

2 The Impact of Low Self-esteem   7

3 How Does Low Self-esteem Develop?   9

4 Connecting the Past and the Present:
   the 'Bottom Line' of Low Self-esteem   15

5 How We Cope with the Bottom Line:
   Rules for Living   19

6 What Keeps Low Self-esteem Going?   21

Part 2: Improving Your Self-esteem   27

7 Identifying Your Bottom Line   29

8 Checking out Negative Predictions   32

9 Questioning Self-critical Thoughts   44

10 Enhancing Self-acceptance   54

11 Changing Your Rules for Living   65

12 Creating a New Bottom Line   73

13 Planning for the Future   82

A Final Word of Encouragement   87
Other Things that Might Help   89
Blank Worksheets   91

About This Book

Why did you pick up this book? The chances are, the title rang bells for you. Perhaps you are aware that you often feel bad about yourself, it's hard to be sure of your own worth, or you find it difficult to approach life with the confidence to be who you truly are – to appreciate yourself and treat yourself with respect and kindness.

Whatever the 'flavour' of your particular kind of low self-esteem, this book is designed to help you to understand how you came to see yourself as you do, and what prevents you from reaching self-acceptance, confidence and healthy self-esteem. It is based on a psychological treatment called cognitive behavioural therapy (CBT), a practical, down-to-earth approach that has a forty-year track record of successfully helping people in distress to transform their lives.

You'll get the most out of the book if, rather than just reading it through, you get stuck in and apply the ideas to yourself. Here's an opportunity to step back and investigate these old ideas about yourself. See if you can bring a kind of friendly curiosity to these investigations. What *is* low self-esteem exactly? How does it affect you? How does it come about? What keeps you stuck in it? What can you do to find a fresh, kinder and more accepting perspective?

You'll find various worksheets you can use to work on important issues. There are copies in the book itself, or you can download them from www. overcoming.co.uk. Or if you prefer you could buy yourself a special notebook in which you can record what you do, and what you learn. Keeping records is really important. It helps new insights and ideas to sink in, makes them easier to remember in the long term, and gives you something to refer back to at those times when perhaps you are tired or stressed and it may be hard to hang on to the changes you have made.

The key thing is to be open-minded and willing to try things – to experiment. The best way of discovering what the book has to offer is to put its ideas into practice in everyday life. Rethinking old attitudes and discovering new ones is an important step. Acting differently and looking at what happens as a result is equally important – in fact, probably more so. The most powerful learning comes from direct experience. So, put yourself in the shoes of the people whose stories we share with you, keep thinking about how the ideas fit your particular circumstances and above all – experiment, experiment, experiment. In doing so, you are making a commitment to yourself and to your future.

The book is designed for you to use on your own. However, if you find that you don't make as much progress as you'd like or would prefer to take a more in-depth approach to your low self-esteem, take a look at the additional resources listed in the *Other Things that Might Help* section at the end of this book. You'll find there a couple of books that go into the ideas in this book in more detail. And if facing up to how you feel about yourself makes you feel worse or is accompanied by serious depression or anxiety or other problems, don't despair. Go to your GP and find out about other ways of approaching the problem – working with a psychological therapist, for example, or even medication.

Good luck!

Melanie Fennell and Lee Brosan

Part 1: UNDERSTANDING LOW SELF-ESTEEM

1

What Is Low Self-esteem?

- *'I never get anything right.'*
- *'I'm no good.'*
- *'I don't deserve anything nice.'*
- *'Other people are better than me.'*
- *'I'm pathetic.'*

Many people think thoughts like these from time to time, perhaps in particular moods or in certain situations. But if this is how you feel about yourself most of the time, and it's hard to see yourself any other way, then you probably suffer from low self-esteem.

'Self-esteem' means the value or worth you place on yourself as a person, your overall *opinion* of yourself. If you have low self-esteem, your opinion of yourself will be negative, and you will not attach much value to yourself as a person. Self-esteem is about the *judgements* that you make of yourself, the way you *evaluate* yourself.

These judgements may be so ingrained that you're not even fully aware of them, but they can have a major impact on how you feel about yourself and how you lead your life.

For the sake of simplicity, we may talk as if you either have low self-esteem or you don't, but it's not really as simple as this. In fact, self-esteem is probably more like weight. Some people are very heavy, and some are very light, and most people are somewhere in between.

Similarly, some people have pretty healthy self-esteem, and perhaps only want to make small changes, but other people's low self-esteem is disabling, and they would like to make much bigger changes. And as with weight, self-esteem can go up and down over the course of your lifetime, according to what is going on in your life, and sometimes according to your mood as well. Whichever is the case for you, you may find in this book ideas that will help you to see yourself in a new, kinder and more accepting light.

Identifying Your Own Low Self-esteem

If you think low self-esteem might be a problem for you, ask yourself these questions:

- *'Do I like myself?'*

- *'Do I accept myself, just as I am, warts and all?'*

- *'Have my experiences in life helped me to appreciate and value myself?'*

- *'Do I look after myself properly and treat myself kindly?'*

- *'Am I able to face challenges without assuming I'll fail?'*

- *'Do I feel it's OK to accept t help from other people?'*

- *'Do I feel it's OK to accept other people's love and attention?'*

- *'Do I expect no more of myself than I do of other people?'*

- *'Do I feel good about myself?'*

If the answer to most of these questions is 'Yes' or 'Yes, most of the time', then it's likely that your self-esteem is pretty healthy. But if you started to clock up more than one or two 'No' or 'Hardly ever' answers, or if you read the sentences and thought 'They must be joking, of course I don't feel like that!', then it's likely that your self-esteem is shaky. On the rating scale below, put an 'X' showing how things stand with you right now.

How do you score? As you go through the book, come back to your rating from time to time, and see if your self-esteem has changed.

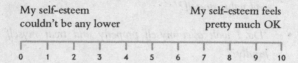

My self-esteem   My self-esteem feels
couldn't be any lower   pretty much OK

2

The Impact of Low Self-esteem

Low self-esteem can affect you in a number of different ways. Do the descriptions below ring true for you?

- *Your thoughts:* You tend to be self-critical and self-blaming, or full of self-doubt. You tend to ignore or discount anything good about yourself, and instead focus on your weaknesses and flaws.

- *Your behaviour:* You may find it difficult to speak up for yourself and spend too much time trying to please others. Or you may feel as if nothing you do is good enough and avoid challenges or drive yourself to perform to a high standard all the time, no matter what the cost. Or perhaps you hide the 'real you', convinced that if others could see you as you really are they would reject you.

- *Your feelings:* Low self-esteem can make you feel sad, hopeless, anxious, guilty, ashamed, or frustrated and angry.

- *Your body:* Low self-esteem can also make you feel drained and tired, or tense and 'uptight'. Avoiding eye contact, speaking very quietly and keeping your head down and your shoulders hunched can all reflect low self-esteem.

- *How you lead your life:* Perhaps, for example, at school or at work you find it difficult to put yourself forward for things, or let other people take the credit for what you have done. Perhaps you spend too much time trying to please other people or feel so frightened of what they might think that you avoid them altogether. Perhaps, in your leisure time, you really want to do something but don't have the confidence to join a club or tackle something challenging – or you may feel that you do not deserve to relax and enjoy yourself. When people's self-esteem is very low, they may even stop taking care of themselves and their appearance. Unfortunately, all of these very understandable patterns will feed into even lower self-esteem.

3

How Does Low Self-esteem Develop?

Let's outline how low self-esteem develops, and
what keeps it going. You'll find the whole process
summarised in the flowchart on page 25. This looks
rather complicated, but don't worry – we'll go
through it step by step, and you'll have a chance
to see how it works in practice, and how it might
apply to you.

This is like a map of the territory of low self-esteem
and shows how everything fits together. Mapping
the territory gives you a sense of how the problem works – how it started, and what is keeping it
going. This is an important step towards learning
that your opinion of yourself is just that – an opinion. Understandable, given your experiences, but
in fact just an idea you picked up a long time ago,
an old unhelpful habit of mind – something you can
learn to stand back from, question and test. You can
learn to say in a more interested, detached way
'Oh, look! There it is again!', to realise that just

because the voice of low self-esteem shouts loudly, it doesn't follow that it tells the truth. And that means you don't have to believe it, feel bad about it, or do what it says.

Josh's Story

Josh was a wanted and loved child, brought up in a reasonably happy, normal family. When he was learning to walk and talk his mum would encourage and praise him. When he went to school and brought home his first reading book she spent time reading with him, and she was really pleased at what he achieved. When he had difficulties or was upset both his parents listened to him and tried to help. So, Josh grew up with a sense that he was worth a lot to his parents, that they liked to give him attention, and that his efforts and his abilities were worthy of praise. If he was naughty then his parents would get cross with him, but never out of proportion to what he had done, and they would set limits or boundaries for him so that he knew what was OK and what wasn't.

Jen's Story

Jen came from a very different family. Her parents were very young when she was born, and they didn't really want to give up their partying lifestyle. They spent a lot of time away from home, passing her from one friend or relative to another, and when they were with her they weren't really interested in what she was doing or how she behaved, as long as she didn't bother them. Jen grew up with the sense that she wasn't wanted, that she was in the way, and that no one was interested or cared for her. If she was naughty her parents would sometimes ignore it, but sometimes they would get furious and scream at her or shut her in her room. So, she never really had a sense of what was acceptable and what wasn't.

Making Sense of Our Stories

We all have our own stories – our own experiences of life – and our ideas and beliefs develop as we try to make sense of them. Josh could make sense of his experience by believing that he was a good and worthwhile person, but Jen could only make sense of her experience by believing that she was unwanted, unlovable and without value to others. In other words, her self-esteem was very low.

Self-esteem Can Be Affected by a Wide Range of Experiences

Different early experiences can lead to low self-esteem – you will find some of them listed below. As you read through the list, notice if any of them ring bells for you. What experiences might have been important in your case?

It's important to realise that it's not just your earliest experiences that can affect self-esteem. If your family was very loving but your first school-teacher didn't like you and picked on you, this could have a big effect on how you feel about yourself. For example, being teased and bullied at any time in your life, whether face to face or online, can have a devastating effect on self-esteem.

Experiences Contributing to Low Self-esteem

Early Experiences

• Being criticised, punished, neglected or abused.

• Failing to meet your parents' standards.

- Being teased, excluded or bullied by other children, including online name-calling or bullying.

- Being compared unfavourably to others.

- Being treated unfairly by others.

- Being on the receiving end of other people's stress or distress.

- Belonging to a family or social group that is a target for prejudice.

- Being the odd one out at home or at school.

- Not having enough of the things you needed in order to develop a secure, healthy sense of self-esteem, such as praise, affection, warmth or interest.

Later Experiences

- Being bullied, intimidated or treated unfairly at work.

- Being abused, physically or emotionally, in relationships.

- Being exposed to persistent stress or hardship.

- Being exposed to traumatic events (such as sexual assault, torture or being in prison).

- Being compared unfavourably to others.

- Losing things that were important to your sense of your worth, for example losing youth, health, good looks or earning capacity.

4

Connecting the Past and the Present: The 'Bottom Line' of Low Self-esteem

As we saw with Josh and Jen, experiences shape our ideas about who we are. We come to general conclusions about ourselves – what we will call the 'Bottom Line' – and they lie at the heart of self-esteem. When our conclusions are generally positive, self-esteem is positive too. So, Josh's Bottom Line was 'I am OK'. But when the conclusions are negative, the result is low self-esteem. So, Jen's Bottom Line was 'I am unwanted and unlovable'.

The trouble with negative Bottom Lines is that they are often formed when you're young, or in very stressful situations. In either case you probably had trouble making fair, realistic and compassionate judgements about what was going on. As a child, Jen saw her parents as attractive, fun, wonderful people to be around. If these wonderful people, who were so nice to their friends, did not like her, she thought it must be because there was something wrong with her, because she was unlovable. It would have been too much to expect her to think, 'My parents behave like this because they are very young and don't want to sacrifice their own pleasures to look after me, and in fact it is them who are to blame, not me.'

Even if you are older when the events that create your Bottom Line happen, it is difficult to weigh them up logically. Why does that teacher dislike you so much and pick on you in class? What's wrong with you? Why do your classmates tease you about your spots, but not bother your friend about hers? Why does your boss keep telling you she has doubts about your work? The simplest explanation is that there must be something wrong with *you*. Your self-esteem needs to be very strong to resist this conclusion.

Sometimes the events that we go through are much more traumatic than those described above. We may be beaten and abused repeatedly, or other terrible things may happen to us. Such events can have a massive impact on how we feel about ourselves, particularly if we believe it's our fault, or we're told that it's what we deserve.

Ways of Thinking that Keep the Bottom Line in Place

We've seen above how the Bottom Line is formed as you try to make sense of what's happening to you. Unfortunately, once the Bottom Line is in place, it starts to affect your everyday thinking. You become 'biased' against yourself, which means that you don't think about yourself fairly and you think that you're to blame, so you stay stuck with low self-esteem. There are two main ways in which your thinking becomes biased.

The first is *a bias in what you pay attention to*. When your self-esteem is low, this sets you up to *notice* things that are in line with your negative views of yourself, and to *ignore or screen out* anything positive. So, when you look in the mirror you see the spot on your cheek and ignore the fact that your hair and your clothes look great. All your shortcomings, flaws and weaknesses jump out and hit you in the face, and all your strengths and good points pass you by.

The second is *a bias in how you weigh up or interpret things around you*. This means that you automatically see the negative side of things. Even if something is clearly positive, the bias can make you see it as negative. So, if a friend pays you a compliment and says you look well, you assume it means that you must normally look pretty bad. Or you might dismiss it by thinking the friend is only saying it to be nice, not because they mean it. You may draw general conclusions about yourself on the basis of small things. For example, if you make a small mistake, you automatically assume it means you're *completely* useless.

These negative ways of thinking keep your Bottom Line alive and active and make it hard to change it since you're continually seeing things in ways that seem to confirm it and ignoring any evidence that would help you to question it and find a fairer and kinder Bottom Line.

5

How We Cope with the Bottom Line: Rules for Living

So, you are stuck with the Bottom Line and don't even question whether it's true or not. You still have to survive as best you can in the world, so you develop 'Rules for Living' to help you get by. Rules tell you how you must act, who you must be, in order to feel at all OK about yourself. So long as you follow your Rules, all is well. But if you fall short, then up comes your Bottom Line. So, obeying your Rules is not a choice – you *have* to do it, no matter what.

For instance, Jen believed that she was unlovable, but she realised that if she was really nice to other people, complimented them and went out of her way to help them, they seemed to like her. So, one of her Rules for Living was, 'In order to be liked, I must always put other people first.' She also spent a lot of time trying to find ways to be more interesting to other people, so that they'd want to be around her. This meant that she didn't have to worry about other people noticing that she was unlovable. Her Rules for Living made it possible for her to function and feel reasonably comfortable around others and OK about herself. Sadly, this example also shows how the Rules for Living can backfire. Because Jen always put other people first, some people grew to expect it and took advantage of her. They would call her for help, but never returned the favour. And because Jen was afraid they wouldn't like her if she stood up for herself, there was nothing to stop them being like that. Being used made Jen feel even more valueless and ended up strengthening her Bottom Line: if people treated her like that, she really *must* be unwanted and unlovable.

6

What Keeps Low Self-esteem Going?

As we've seen, experience leads to the Bottom
Line, and this in turn leads to the Rules for Living
that help you to cope. The Bottom Line can affect
you in two big ways. Firstly, it makes you *anxious
and worried that something may go wrong*: your Rules
for Living may not work, and you and everyone
else will see just how true the Bottom Line is.
So, naturally, *you take precautions* to stop this from
happening. This is the chain of events on the right-
hand side of the low self-esteem vicious circle at
the bottom of the flowchart on page 25. The left-
hand side of the vicious circle shows what happens
when you think that things *have* gone wrong, and
the Bottom Line *has* been confirmed: you become
self-critical and your mood drops. Notice that, generally speaking, fear and worry are about events that
might happen in the future, while self-criticism and
low mood tend to be about things that have already
happened in the past.

Let's look at Jen's story. As we do so, notice if anything rings bells for you. How might this vicious circle apply to you?

How Low Self-Esteem Develops and What Keeps It Going: Jen's Chart

Here we describe, first of all in words and then in a flowchart, how Jen's low self-esteem creates a vicious circle. She has been invited to her firm's office party in a swanky hotel:

Negative Predictions and Anxiety

(the right-hand side of the low self-esteem vicious circle in the flowchart)

Remember Jen's Bottom Line was 'I am unwanted and unlovable', so her first thought was, 'There's no point going, no one will talk to me, and if they do I'll just make a complete fool of myself.' She *makes negative predictions* about how things will go. And because she really believes her predictions, she feels very anxious. It seems there are only two courses of action open to her: to avoid the whole thing, or to take precautions to stop her negative predictions from coming true − for example, to go but try to make herself super-interesting in some way.

Suppose she decided not to go to the party, she might at first feel a sense of relief. But imagine what might happen next. Next day in the office, when everyone is chatting and laughing about the party, Jen can't join in and ends up feeling isolated and excluded. Once again, she has confirmed her Bottom Line.

On the other hand, suppose she goes but makes huge efforts to make herself interesting so people will want to talk to her. She spends a lot of time swotting up on international issues – the politics of the day, the climate crisis, the latest news on GM crops. And at the party she thinks 'I'd better not drink, or I won't remember any of this.' The party gets going, and everyone is drinking and gossiping. But when Jen talks to people, they seem to wander off and avoid her. Serious conversation isn't what they're looking for! So, yet again, poor Jen has confirmed her Bottom Line. She can't see that her efforts to stop her predictions from coming true in fact produced just the results she dreaded and concludes that next time she'll have to try even harder.

As you can see, the problem with both of these strategies is that they stop Jen discovering that her Bottom Line and her Rules for Living may not be true or useful. Maybe if she allowed herself to be spontaneous and natural, all would be well. It could be that in fact she's fine, just as she is.

Self-criticism and Depression

(the left-hand side of the low self-esteem vicious circle)

The process does not stop with confirmation of the Bottom Line. Often a spate of *self-critical thoughts* follows. Jen told herself, 'I'm such an idiot, why did I bother? I'm so boring and stupid, no one will ever want me.' Understandably, once you start criticising yourself, your mood drops. This is you, this is who you are. You start to feel hopeless. And then your self-critical thoughts get even stronger. Critical thoughts and low mood feed the Bottom Line and keep it active. You feel worse and worse about yourself and, of course, when you face your next challenge, you will once again anticipate the worst.

How Is All This Relevant to You?

On page 93, you'll find a 'fill in the blanks' version of the flowchart illustrating how low self-esteem works (this is also available for download at www. overcoming.co.uk). Now is the moment to use these ideas to map out how things are for you personally. The best starting point is a recent time when you felt anxious and uncertain – a time that is still fresh in your mind, so you can remember it

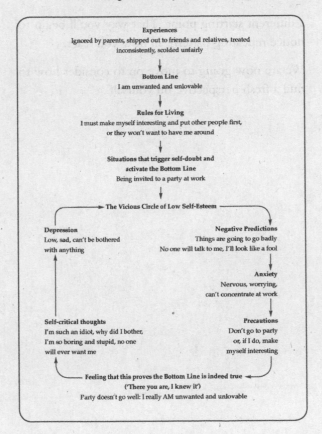

Experiences
Ignored by parents, shipped out to friends and relatives, treated
inconsistently, scolded unfairly

Bottom Line
I am unwanted and unlovable

Rules for Living
I must make myself interesting and put other people first,
or they won't want to have me around

**Situations that trigger self-doubt and
activate the Bottom Line**
Being invited to a party at work

The Vicious Circle of Low Self-Esteem

Depression
Low, sad, can't be bothered
with anything

Negative Predictions
Things are going to go badly
No one will talk to me, I'll look like a fool

Anxiety
Nervous, worrying,
can't concentrate at work

Self-critical thoughts
I'm such an idiot, why did I bother,
I'm so boring and stupid, no one
will ever want me

Precautions
Don't go to party
or, if I do, make
myself interesting

Feeling that this proves the Bottom Line is indeed true
('There you are, I knew it')
Party doesn't go well: I really AM unwanted and unlovable

clearly. See if you can get curious about your reactions at each stage – become your own detective and ferret them out. In fact, it may be helpful to map out more than one vicious circle, each with a different starting point. That way you'll begin to notice repeating patterns in how you react.

We are now going to move on to consider how to find a fresh perspective on yourself.

Part 2: IMPROVING YOUR SELF-ESTEEM

In Part 2, we'll look at some practical ways of tackling the self-defeating patterns of thought and behaviour that keep low self-esteem going. These patterns prevent you from updating your old, negative Bottom Line and finding more realistic and helpful Rules for Living. Three core skills are central to your journey to healthy self-esteem. They are:

1. **Awareness** (close observation of your day-to-day experiences and reactions, especially the thinking that feeds your low self-esteem).

2. **Rethinking** (learning to step back, to question unhelpful thoughts, Rules and your Bottom Line and to find kinder, more helpful alternatives).

3. **Experiments** (checking out old and new perspectives through direct experience of new ways of operating).

Time now to put these skills into practice, to learn to be your own good friend, accepting and valuing yourself just as you are.

7

Identifying
Your Bottom Line

In Part 1, we asked you to think about what experiences in your life might have shaped how you feel about yourself. Now it's time to pinpoint your Bottom Line. What messages did your experiences give you about yourself, while you were growing up and perhaps later in your life? How did they teach you to judge yourself? What do you say about yourself when you are being self-critical? What names did other people call you if they were angry or disappointed?

If you could sum up the heart of your doubts about yourself in a single sentence beginning with the words 'I am . . .', what would it be? Try to finish the sentence below – don't think about it too much, just write down the first thing that comes to mind. You may find just one Bottom Line comes to mind, or you may discover more than one.

'I am_____

_____

_____

_____

_____

_____

_____

_____'

It is extremely important to understand that your Bottom Line is an *opinion based on your experiences*, not a true statement about you. But what experiences exactly? Ask yourself when you *first* felt about yourself as you do now. What memories come to mind? If these are of a time early in your life, there may also be more recent experiences that have strengthened your poor opinion of yourself. If so, add them to your list.

'The experiences that seem to be connected to my Bottom Line are _____

_____

_____

_____

_____

_____

_____

_____

_____,

Later in this section, we'll look at how to change your Rules for Living and create a new Bottom Line, but first we'll show you how to tackle the day-to-day thinking that keeps them going – negative predictions and self-criticism.

8

Checking out Negative Predictions

(tackling the right-hand side of
the low self-esteem vicious circle)

We saw in Part 1 that certain situations can *activate
your Bottom Line* – you have the feeling that your
Rules for Living are about to be broken, and you start
to make *negative predictions*. Something's going to go
wrong. *Anxiety* – a sense that you are under threat –
is your clue that this is happening. Naturally enough,
you want to stop your predictions from coming true,
and that's where *taking precautions* comes in. In the
short term, your precautions may be helpful – they
give you the sense that you have managed to avoid
disaster. But in the longer term, they are unhelpful
in two ways. Firstly, if things do go well for you, you
assume it's because of your precautions. You have
no chance to discover whether you really needed
them or not, and that things might have gone OK
without them. This means you never find out if your
predictions really would have come true. Secondly,
precautions can sometimes make things worse.

Tackling your negative predictions involves four key steps:

1. Identifying the predictions and the precautions you take to stop them from coming true (awareness);

2. Questioning your predictions and looking for an alternative view (rethinking);

3. Taking action to check out how accurate your predictions are by dropping your precautions (experiments);

4. Using the results of your experiments to come up with new predictions, decide whether you really needed those precautions or not, and work out what to do next.

We'll take each of these steps in turn, and you'll have a chance to try them out for yourself, using the worksheets on pages 94 and 96 or online at www.overcoming.co.uk. This will help you to take it step by step and learn new skills systematically – the most helpful way of breaking old self-defeating habits. It's not usually helpful to think about these things in very general terms – what you learn can stay rather vague and be hard to put into practice. So, start by choosing a specific situation to work with, something current, and ideally an example of a difficulty that you often face. You can then use what you learn to deal with other anxieties about yourself.

Let's look at each of the four key steps in detail. We'll use the example of Matt to show how the exercise can work. Matt's father was always very critical when he was growing up, and nothing was ever good enough for him. Matt's Bottom Line is 'I'm not good enough'; one of his Rules for Living is 'I must always do everything brilliantly, or else I will be attacked and punished.' As a result, he works very hard and makes sure that he's always very well prepared for everything. Now he has been asked to give an important presentation at work the next day (something he is actually good at), on something crucial to his team's success.

STEP 1:

Identify your predictions and the precautions you take to stop them coming true as precisely as you can (Awareness)

Predictions

It's important to be really clear about what you think will happen, whether you experience your predictions as words or as images. Otherwise you'll have trouble working out if you were right – or not. Matt's prediction was:

I'll completely mess this up, and I'll probably end up getting the sack. I'm not good enough to do this, and no one's going to support me – they'll all have a go at me if I don't do it right. I can see their faces now.

It's possible that Matt is overestimating the chances that something will go wrong, and how bad it will be if it does go wrong, and that he's underestimating his ability to cope with the challenge and the likelihood that people will be willing to support him. These are negative predictions.

Precautions

What do you do to stop your predictions from coming true? As we've seen, if you carry on taking precautions, you'll never find out whether the predictions are valid or not.

Matt looked at masses of books and websites to try and cover every angle of the topic before the talk. He stayed up for most of the night trying to prepare very thoroughly. In fact, although he was very tired, the presentation went well. His colleagues supported him and cheered at the end. He was aware that he'd already known most of the things that he was asked, and that he'd spent hours swotting up on things that he was never asked about, but he told himself, 'It was just as well – if I hadn't been up all night someone might have asked something I couldn't answer and they'd have realised that I'm not good enough for this job.' So, Matt never learned to trust his skills and his experience, and his belief that he wasn't really good enough continued.

STEP 2:

Questioning your predictions and looking for an alternative view (Rethinking)

Now that you have identified your negative predictions and precautions, the next stage is to step back and question the predictions. You can use these questions to help:

- What evidence *supports* what I'm predicting – how do I KNOW what will happen?

- Is there any evidence *against* what I'm predicting?

- What's the worst that can happen? How likely is this?

- If the worst really does happen, what can I do to cope or make it better?

- What help and resources can I tap into?

- What's the best that can happen? Is it possible that things could go well?

- Realistically, what's most likely to happen?

- What alternative views are there? Is there any evidence for these?

Often it's easier when trying to come up with questions and alternatives to imagine that you are talking to a friend. What would you say to a friend who had the same thoughts as you do? Would you say, 'Yes, I expect you're right, it will all go horribly wrong'? You probably wouldn't, but would be able to come up with a lot of suggestions. Or imagine what a friend might say to you if you could bring yourself to tell them about your fears.

Matt, for instance, might have come up with these alternatives:

I do really know my stuff – I've worked here for a while and I know they think I'm OK. The boss wouldn't have asked me to do it if he didn't have some faith in me after all. And actually, he has said that I'm good at thinking on my feet in meetings! If only I could believe it! I'll make a list of all the times I can remember when I did think on my feet and it was OK.

STEP 3:

Take action to check out how accurate your predictions are by dropping your precautions (Experiments)

Here's your chance to experiment with a new way of doing things. What happens if you *don't* take precautions? You may discover to your surprise that they were quite unnecessary – you were OK without them. Doing an experiment like this will also help you judge whether your new alternative perspective is useful as it stands, or whether it needs further thought.

Some practical tips:

* Be clear about exactly how you'll *know for a fact* if your prediction comes true. What will tell you that it is true? Or that it isn't?

* Make sure that you don't use *any* of your precautions. It'll feel very scary to go into a situation without them, but it's the only way to discover the truth about your predictions.

* Work out what you'll do instead of using the precautions. It's important to decide what you *will* do, not just what you will stop doing – otherwise you may feel at a loss when you find yourself in the situation. For example, if

avoiding eye contact is one of your precautions, work out what you'll do instead (for instance, look at people for brief periods as you speak).

• Take time to think about the results of your experiment. How did you manage without the precautions? Did the things that you were afraid of come true?

Matt's experiment next time he was asked to give a presentation was that for once he would not prepare too much. He'd remind himself of the major points he needed to cover, and then do something completely different to take his mind off the whole business. The next morning when the meeting took place, he was very nervous at first, but he reminded himself that this was an experiment and that he was going to approach it like that. In fact, the meeting did go OK. He did a good presentation, and although the client was in a horrible mood and kept niggling him about details, he kept his cool and dealt with the queries. His colleagues were very supportive about the client, and about the way that he handled it.

Matt realised that if he had prepared a lot, he'd have thought his success was due to the preparation, not to his natural talent for the business. He realised that actually he didn't need to do much preparation at all.

When Precautions Make Things Worse

We can also use Matt to show how precautions can sometimes make things worse. Imagine he went home and spent all night preparing. Next day he's so tired that, although he knows everything, he can barely keep his eyes open during the presentation. As a result, it goes quite badly, and his boss is annoyed. His precautions have made things worse for him, not better. He hasn't learned to trust his skills and his experience, and his belief that he isn't good enough and the pressure to try too hard will continue.

STEP 4:

Reviewing your results and working out what to do next

Before you do anything else, congratulate yourself on what you have done. Whatever the results were, doing an experiment takes courage and determination. Then it's time to review your results, come up with new predictions based on what you've learned, decide whether you really need those precautions, and work out what to do next.

If your prediction didn't come true when you dropped your precautions, you will have had a chance to realise that maybe you don't need them.

You've discovered that change is possible. Matt's experiment gave him a new belief: 'Maybe I *am* good enough!' The next time he was asked, he was much more willing to predict that everything would go OK.

But if your prediction *did* come true, do not despair. There may be good reasons why this happened.

Suppose, after Matt had done only a small amount of preparation, the presentation didn't go well. It could be that he really isn't good enough – but there could be other reasons. It may have been his anxiety, not the lack of preparation, that caused the problem. Or it may have been that the client was in a vile mood and was trying to trip him up, and no amount of preparation would have helped. It could also have been that, even though things didn't go as well as he'd have liked, they weren't catastrophic. Perhaps everybody was sympathetic, and he didn't get the sack. So even if things didn't work out as he hoped, he could have thought, 'It wouldn't have made much difference if I'd prepared for a year, and people seemed to be really sympathetic and said I'd done a good job.' Then, the next time he was asked to do something, he could tell himself, 'It didn't go brilliantly last time, but it wasn't because of the preparation – I knew my stuff. Whatever happens this time, I'll probably be fine, and I'll probably learn something useful, however it turns out.'

Once you have identified some new, more realistic predictions, make a note of them. The next time you encounter the same situation, act as if they were true, even if you still have some doubts, and see what happens. In a more general sense, ask yourself what you've learned from your experiment, and where you need to go next. It's very unlikely that one single experiment will rid you of anxiety. Changing old habits takes time. So, do you need a repeat? Or are you ready to take on a slightly more challenging situation? Or perhaps it's time to apply what you've learned to a new situation? Whatever you decide, remember that this work is an important foundation for updating your Rules for Living and your Bottom Line.

Recording How You Tackle Negative Predictions

The process we have described can be recorded on the record sheet shown opposite. We have shown Matt as an example and there's a blank form at the end of the book for you to copy, or you could of course download it from www.overcoming.co.uk. That way you can keep a record of your own work.

Predictions and Precautions Record Sheet

Date/time	Situation What were you doing when you began to feel anxious?	Emotions and body sensations (e.g. anxious, panicky, tense) Rate 0–10 for how bad it was	Negative predictions What exactly was going through your mind (e.g. thoughts in words, images)? Rate each one 0–10 for how much you believed it	Precautions What did you do to stop your predictions from coming true (e.g. avoid the situation, take precautions)?	Alternative perspectives Use the questions in Step 2 to find other views of the situation. Rate each one 0–10 for how much you believe it	Experiment What did you do instead of taking your usual precautions? What were the results? What did you learn?
Mon 4.30 p.m.	Boss asked me to do a presentation THE NEXT DAY!!!!	Panicky, terrified, want to run away: *9/10*	I can't do this; he should know I can't, and I won't have time to prepare. I will blow it; they'll all know that I'm a fraud and an idiot: *8/10*	I'm just going to have to take everything home and work all night. I can't risk going unprepared.	My boss wouldn't have asked if he didn't think I could do it. He thinks I'm good at thinking on my feet! I don't need to prepare that much – in fact if I do then I'll just get tired and worn out: About *6/10?*	Spent a little time preparing, but then watched TV and chatted to Ben. Presentation went much better than I'd thought it would. Maybe I don't need to prepare so much?!!!

9

Questioning Self-critical Thoughts

We've seen that people with low self-esteem are hard on themselves. Sometimes without even realising that they are doing it, they call themselves names, put themselves down and blame themselves when things go wrong. They notice every weakness and failure and berate themselves as a result.

We're talking now about the left-hand side of the low self-esteem vicious circle in the flowchart on page 25. When it seems the Bottom Line is true, we become self-critical. Self-critical thoughts make us feel low, and feeling low in turn produces even more negative thoughts and keeps the Bottom Line active. In this section, you will have a chance to use the core skills you have already practised to develop a more balanced and kinder view of yourself.

What's the effect of self-criticism? Read the list of words below slowly and carefully, allowing each one to sink in. Imagine that they're accurate descriptions of you:

Useless	Unattractive	Incompetent
Weak	Unlikeable	Ugly
Pathetic	Unwanted	Stupid
Worthless	Inferior	Inadequate

What was the impact on your confidence and your mood of reading those words? Just thinking about these words in connection with yourself may well have made you feel bad.

Now imagine a little girl whose older sister becomes jealous as she starts to grow up. The older sister makes comments all the time – you look stupid, they're laughing at you, no one likes you, you did that all wrong. What effect do you think this stream of criticism would have on the little girl? After a while she'd feel very bad about herself. This is exactly how *self*-criticism works. If you put yourself down, it will affect you just as much as if someone else was doing it. And notice how you felt about the older sister, too. Did you think her behaviour was justified? Even without knowing anything about either of them, you probably wanted to tell her to back off, stop being so mean, and leave the little one alone. In this section you'll find out how to do this for yourself as well.

Many people think self-criticism is a good thing. It helps to keep standards up, and stops you becoming vain or smug or boastful. But in fact, you don't need to criticise yourself to keep standards up. People tend to respond much better to praise than to criticism, even from themselves. And if you genuinely like yourself then you're much less likely to be vain and smug than someone who's trying to cover up feeling bad. Self-criticism isn't necessary, and it certainly isn't helpful. In fact, quite the reverse. It's unfair, it kicks you when you're down and it stops you from making constructive changes. Time to let it go!

Dealing with self-critical thoughts involves a number of key steps, which use the same core skills as checking out negative predictions:

1. Learning to spot the thoughts as they happen (awareness).

2. Learning to question them and come up with alternatives (rethinking).

3. Behaving in line with your new perspective – treating yourself with respect, acceptance and kindness (experiments).

STEP 1: Learning to Spot Self-critical Thoughts

As with learning to spot anxious predictions, the first step in stopping self-critical thoughts is to become aware of them as they happen. This may be difficult if you've been having them for so long that they're just part of your mental furniture — a habit so well established that you don't even realise they're there.

Using the first part of the 'Dealing with Self-critical Thoughts' form shown at the end of this section is a good way to start. We have completed the form to show you an example of how to fill it out, and there is a blank form at the end of the book for you to try it yourself (p.94) and of course, you may choose to download it. The form asks you to write down a situation in which you began to criticise yourself, your exact thoughts, and the emotions and body sensations that went with them.

Your self-critical thoughts may be in words, or they may take the form of pictures or images. If so, just make a note of the content of the images, and what they mean (for example, an image of yourself looking hunched and red in the face might mean that you think you just made a fool of yourself and everyone noticed). Often self-critical thinking produces a recognisable pattern of feelings and sensations in your body. So every time you notice that your mood drops a little, or you feel down on yourself, or you have that familiar sinking feeling in your stomach, stop and ask: 'Have I just had a self-critical thought?' Or you could set your watch or mobile phone to beep once an hour. When it goes off ask yourself, 'Have I thought anything self-critical in the last few minutes?' As time goes on and you get more practised, it will be easier to notice the thoughts as they occur.

STEP 2: Learning to Question Self-critical Thoughts and Find Alternatives

Just as you learned to question your negative predictions, so you can learn to question your self-critical thoughts and search for fairer, kinder and more encouraging alternative perspectives. Here are some questions to help in your search.

Question: What is the evidence?

- Am I confusing a thought with a fact?

- What is the evidence that supports what I think about myself?

- What is the evidence that contradicts what I think about myself?

Question: What alternative views are there?

- Am I assuming that my view is the only one possible?

- What evidence do I have to support alternative views?

Question: What is the effect of thinking the way I do about myself?

• Does thinking like this make me behave in self-defeating ways?

• What alternative might lead to a more constructive course of action?

Question: What are the unfair ways I am thinking about myself?

• Am I jumping to conclusions?

• Am I using a double standard — one for me and a different one for everyone else?

• Am I thinking in all-or-nothing terms — if it's not perfect then it must be awful?

• Am I condemning myself as a total person because of one small thing?

• Am I concentrating on my weaknesses and forgetting my strengths?

• Am I blaming myself for things that aren't my fault?

• Am I expecting myself to be perfect?

Question: What can I do?

• How can I put a new, kinder view into practice?

- Is there anything that I can do to change the situation? If not, what can I do to think differently about it in the future?

- How can I experiment with acting in a less self-defeating way?

The most important of all these questions is, 'Am I confusing a thought with a fact?' It's easy to mistake your self-critical thoughts for factual statements about yourself, especially if you've had them for a very long time and they feel like part of you. But just because you believe something to be true, it *does not mean that it is*. For instance, supposing for some reason you came to believe that you were a giraffe. Would that make you one? The first step is to realise that thoughts are just thoughts – it's only when we find evidence to back them up that we can say that they are facts.

One useful trick is to imagine that you are trying to convince a jury in a court of law. The jury will not accept something as true just because a witness says they believe it – they need evidence.

STEP 3: Behaving in Line with Your New Perspective

Once you have found some kinder alternatives to your self-critical thoughts, it's time to start acting as if they were true. If you believed your new alternatives, what would you do differently? Ask yourself how someone who truly believed your new alternatives would behave, and see if you can behave that way too, even if you're not yet fully convinced that your alternatives are true. The more you put them into practice, the more convincing your alternatives will become. Make a note of what happens when you act in this new way. Which works better for you – the self-defeating route, or the new, constructive route?

Question: What can I do?

- How can I put my new perspective into practice and treat myself more kindly?

- Is there anything that I can do to change the situation that sparked off my self-critical thinking? If not, what can I do to think differently about it in the future?

- How can I experiment with acting in less self-defeating ways?

Chloe's Story

Chloe was a young woman who was filled with anxiety and self-doubt. She was an only child brought up alone by a young mother. When Chloe was seven, her mother married a man who later said that he didn't want children. He made it clear that he didn't want Chloe around. She wasn't allowed into the living room and had to spend most of her time in her bedroom. At meals her stepfather would pick on her and criticise her, telling her that as far as he was concerned she was lucky to have anything to eat and had no right to anything in the house. If she or her mother tried to stand up for her, her stepfather would tell her that she was a waste of space who didn't deserve anything. Her Bottom Line was 'I'm not worthy of anything', and her Rules for Living were that she had to accept anything that happened to her without making a fuss, or she would only make things worse. Sadly, but not surprisingly, as an adult Chloe hooked up with a friend who genuinely liked her but took advantage of her. The next table shows how Chloe dealt with her self-critical thoughts.

Dealing with Self-critical Thoughts

Date/ time	Situation What were you doing when you began to feel bad about yourself?	Emotions and body sensations (e.g. sad, angry, tense, stomach churning). Rate how bad each was 0–10	Self-critical thoughts What exactly was going through your mind when you started to feel bad about yourself? How far did you believe each thought? (Rate 0–10)	Alternative perspectives Use the questions in Step 2 to find other ways of seeing yourself. Rate belief in each (0–10)	Outcome 1. How do you feel after coming up with alternatives (0–10)? 2. How far do you now believe the critical thoughts (0–10)? 3. What can you do now (action plan, experiment)?
Friday evening	Meg asked if she could borrow my new coat – which I haven't worn yet. I knew that she wouldn't take care of it properly, but I lent it to her anyway.	Ashamed, angry with myself, 8/10. Depressed, 8/10.	I didn't want to lend it to her, but I didn't dare say 'No' in case she turned on me. I'm such a stupid wimp but I just couldn't do it – I'm so weak and pathetic! I'll never be able to do anything different, my stepfather was right – I'm a waste of space. 10/10.	I'm not really pathetic – I have a very good reason for feeling as I do, and anyone would be likely to feel the same. My stepfather was NOT right – he's the reason I think like this! 9/10.	1. Feel a bit better – it's good to remind myself of how all this started. 2. Hmm . . . About 2–3/10. 3. Take the risk next time someone asks something unreasonable and say 'No'. Tell Meg I'm upset about the coat and ask her to get it cleaned. I think she'll be OK about it – she did apologise.

10

Enhancing Self-acceptance

We have seen how people with low self-esteem think in an unfair way about themselves and easily home in on anything that confirms their bad view of themselves. In the last section, you learned how to question self-critical thinking, to find new, kinder and fairer perspectives and to begin to think about how best to put them into practice. Now you can take your learning a step further, discovering a more balanced view of yourself not only by being less self-critical, but also by bringing your good qualities into focus (awareness, rethinking), and learning to treat yourself with respect, consideration and kindness (experiments). Let us take each of these in turn.

Cultivating a Balanced View of Yourself

The idea here is to start intentionally noticing the good things about you. This may sound simple, but in practice it can be very difficult. For one thing,

old habits are hard to break. If you've been thinking something for a long time it's difficult to start
thinking in a different way. Practice makes it much
easier, but don't be surprised if you find it hard at
first and take a while to get the hang of it.

It can be hard to think well of ourselves and to
acknowledge our good points because we're scared
what people will think of us if we're too positive.
This can affect everyone, not just people with low
self-esteem – it's something to do with our culture.
We could call it a ban or 'taboo' on thinking well of
ourselves. Look at the following statements:

- *'I'm beautiful.'*

- *'I'm clever.'*

- *'I'm just so adorable.'*

- *'I'm a brilliant cook.'*

If you heard someone saying these things what
would your first thought be? Something along
the lines of 'Who does she think she is?' or 'How
vain can you get!'? We tend to frown on people
who 'blow their own trumpet', 'boast' or generally
speak well of themselves. In order to allow yourself to think good things about yourself, you must
remember that accepting yourself as you are and
appreciating your good qualities is very different

from boasting. Allowing yourself to see your good side is not vain and smug – it's fair! You don't have to go over the top and think everything about you is brilliant, but you do need to allow yourself a balanced view.

There are three key steps that you can take to enhance your self-acceptance:

1. Bringing your strengths and good qualities into focus.

2. Using a list of your strengths and good qualities to create a new view of yourself.

3. Strengthening this new view by creating a 'Positives Portfolio', a daily record of examples of your strengths and good qualities in action.

STEP 1: Bringing Your Strengths and Good Qualities into Focus

If your self-esteem has been low for a very long time, then at first, it'll probably be hard to find anything good about yourself. Don't be discouraged if it is difficult – this is natural, and learning to be as kind to yourself as you would to another person you cared about needs time and practice. The questions below may help you to make a start.

Questions to Help You Identify Your Good Points

Write down what comes to mind as you reflect on the questions below. As you do so, watch out for thinking, 'Yes, but . . .', because this stops you from accepting what comes to mind. 'Yes, buts . . .', are like self-critical thoughts, so allow yourself to put them on one side instead of believing them and being put off by them.

- What do you like about yourself, however unimportant it may seem?

- What positive qualities do you possess?

- What have you achieved this week, however small?

- What have you achieved at any point in your life, however small?

- What challenges have you faced?

- What gifts or talents do you have, however modest?

- What skills have you acquired?

- What do other people seem to like or value in you?

- What qualities and actions do you value in other people and think you might share?

- What aspects of yourself would you appreciate if they were aspects of another person?

- What small positives are you ignoring?

- What are the bad things you are *not*?

- How might someone who cared about you describe you?

If you still find it hard to think of anything, you may be tempted to have more self-critical thoughts like, 'The reason I can't think of anything is because there just isn't anything good about me.' Or you may find that you've only come up with a few positive things, and have self-critical thoughts like: 'Is that it? There's so little. That's really pathetic – it just proves how useless I am.' Remember that these thoughts are just thoughts. You can't think of anything because your old habits of mind and the strength of your Bottom Line stop you from seeing your strong points – not because they are not there. If you persist with these techniques, then the Bottom Line itself may start to change.

STEP 2: Using Your List of Good Qualities to Create a New View of Yourself

Reliving your good qualities in action

Once you've started to make your list, make sure

you keep it close to hand. Don't just put it away and forget about it. Give yourself a few more days to add other things that might come to mind, and then find somewhere quiet and relaxing to read the list through. Read it slowly, consider each item, let it sink in, and bring to mind a particular time when you showed that quality in your actions. Let yourself remember this in detail, almost as if you were living it all over again – what you could see at the time, what you could hear, touch, taste and smell, what you did and what happened then. See if you can call up the feelings you had at the time. The more vividly you recall these memories, the more real that quality will start to seem.

As you do this, you may well notice thoughts that say, 'This is just rubbish, it's not really me.' This is just your old habit of self-critical thinking. You do not need to pay attention to such thoughts, or to give them any weight. Instead, put them to one side or, if you need to, write them down (using the worksheet from the previous section), question them, and work out more constructive alternatives that, rather than getting in your way, will help you to continue your journey towards self-acceptance.

STEP 3: Routine Awareness of Your Good Points: Your 'Positives Portfolio'

The next step is to try and be aware of your good points every single day. This may seem strange at first, but after a while it should start to come more naturally and automatically, and you won't need to do it deliberately. You are learning to be fair to yourself, to make recognising your good points as strong a habit as focusing on your weaknesses has been up until now. Start by aiming to write down three examples of good points every day – or if three is too many, then start with one or two. It's different for everybody. For each entry, write down whatever you did in enough detail to be able to remember it later, and note the quality that it shows. You'll then have a record you can look back over, especially at times when you're feeling low or stressed or unconfident.

Jen, whose story we looked at near the beginning of this book, is now married with three children. Although her husband and family love her, the effect of her childhood means that she still has very low self-esteem. Her list of good points about herself started like this:

- *Wrote a report at work – Persevering; competent.*

- *Cooked daughter's favourite meal when she finished exams – Thoughtful.*

- *Put up shelf when husband was away — Hooray, practical!*

Once you find you can easily record up to three items every day, up your game. Move to four, and then perhaps five or more, until it becomes completely automatic for you to recognise and value examples of your good points — they have become part of your mental furniture. At this point, you have no further need to write them down.

Learning to Enjoy Yourself and Treat Yourself Kindly

When your self-esteem is low, it is easy to think that you don't deserve to relax or enjoy yourself, and to feel that nothing you do is good enough. Part of cultivating low self-esteem is to learn to treat yourself more fairly and kindly, to learn to be your own good friend, accepting and valuing yourself just as you are. This has two aspects: enriching your life with pleasures and treats, and giving yourself credit for your successes and achievements.

STEP 1: Enjoyment: Enriching Your Life with Pleasures and Treats

Are you aware of any thoughts or Rules that get in your way when you consider taking time to relax and enjoy yourself? Perhaps you feel you have to look after everyone else first, that you don't deserve nice things in your life, or that pleasure has to be earned. Here is a chance to become aware of such ideas when they come up and get in your way, to rethink them, and to experiment with a new approach.

A good start is to keep a diary for a week, and every day jot down the things you do. Make a note of how much you enjoyed each activity by giving it a rating between 0 (not at all) and 10 (a lot). At the end of the week, look back over your ratings. What have you enjoyed doing, even if only a bit? What have you really, really enjoyed?

You can build on what's already working for you, and make a list of all the things you'd *like to do*, activities you find enjoyable or relaxing, and treats that you could give yourself. Don't hold back – write down things that even seem crazy and unrealistic, too expensive or too fattening, as well as smaller and more easily obtainable things. Notice if the thoughts that make this difficult try to get in the way and see if you can put them to one side or, if you need to, rethink them.

For example, Jen's list was:

* *Buy some really nice aromatherapy bath oil and soak in the bath for ages.*

- *Persuade my husband to take me to Greece – I've always wanted to go.*

- *Buy a really nice bottle of red wine and drink it whilst watching a DVD with my husband.*

- *Take the kids to see the new film they've asked about, and for a pizza afterwards.*

- *Have a Mars bar.*

- *Take the time to exercise properly three times a week even if it means not doing what someone else wants me to do at that time.*

- *Spend half an hour a day reading.*

- *Find out about parachuting!!!*

Keep your list somewhere easy to get hold of and add to it whenever you think of new things you'd like. Make sure you act on the list too – that's what will make the difference. Aim to do at least one small thing for yourself every day. Week by week, you can then plan to add more things you enjoy and more treats for yourself into your life, day by day.

STEP 2: Achievement: Learning to Treat Yourself Fairly

You can use the same method to prove to yourself that you aren't useless at everything and in fact accomplish much more than you thought. This time, rate each activity you write down according to how much of an accomplishment it was, from 0 (not an accomplishment at all) to 10 (a really big accomplishment). Make sure you include small things like managing to scrape the burnt bits off the roasting tin! And it's really important to take account of how you felt at the time. For example, something everyday (like making the dinner) might be easy if you are feeling fine, but a real achievement if you are tired or stressed. If you don't recognise this, you risk being unfair to yourself. Sometimes even simple things can take real effort and are worth a pat on the back.

Again, at the end of the week, look back at what you've done and how much satisfaction and sense of accomplishment you got from it. You can use this as the basis for adding more of these activities into your life. Watch out for self-critical thoughts that try to undermine your sense of accomplishment ('Any fool could have done that' or 'Why didn't you do that better?'). See if you can put them to one side and continue in spite of them or, if you need to, write them down, question them and find a more helpful, fairer way of looking at what you have achieved.

11

Changing Your Rules for Living

As we said earlier, our Rules for Living are ways of coping with the Bottom Line. They allow you to try and get around the Bottom Line, but they leave it unchanged instead of encouraging you to question it. So, they just wallpaper over what you really feel about yourself.

Rules for Living are usually easy to spot because they tend to be expressed in terms of 'shoulds' or 'oughts' or 'musts'. Chloe's Rule was: 'I must never try to stick up for myself or I'll make things worse.'

You can use the same core skills you have already practised when working with anxious predictions and self-critical thoughts to change your Rules. This involves three key steps:

1. Identifying your Rules and assessing their impact on your life (awareness).

2. Questioning your Rules and finding new ones (rethinking).

3. Putting your new Rules into practice (experiments).

STEP 1: Identifying Your Rules and Their Impact on Your Life

What Are Your Rules?

- If you've kept notes on your anxious predictions and self-critical thoughts, look through them and see if you can find themes that seem to come up again and again. What kind of situations make you doubt yourself or think badly of yourself? For instance, someone may have made a small criticism of something you've done, and now you think you're useless. Does this reflect a Rule that you have to be perfect in order to be acceptable? If you notice repeated patterns, might these be reflections of your underlying Rules?

- Consider when you criticise yourself. Self-criticism often follows thinking that we have not lived up to our Rules.

- Think about your earlier experiences. Rules are often rooted in early life. They may have been ideas and values that were there in the household that you grew up in. What messages were you given about how to behave, and the sort of person you should be? We'll come back to this a little later.

- Think about what makes you feel really, really good! Often we feel great when we have successfully done just what our Rules tell us we should.

Once you have a sense of what your Rules are, write them down.

What Is the Impact of Your Rules?

Rules for Living don't just pop into our heads in specific situations but lurk at the back of our minds and influence how we think, feel and act in a whole range of situations. Once you have identified a Rule, it's worth considering the impact it's had on your life. Often our Rules, which we developed to help us through life, actually make life more difficult for us.

Ask yourself the following questions, and make a note of your answers:

- How does the Rule affect my relationships? My work? My studies? My leisure?

- How does it affect how well I cope when things go wrong?

- Has it made me expect more of myself than is reasonable for any normal human being?

- Have I missed out on things, or failed to take advantage of opportunities, because of it?

STEP 2: Questioning Your Rules and Finding Alternatives

Rules for Living have often been in place for a long time and had a powerful effect on your life. So, changing them will not happen overnight. But becoming aware of them, and understanding their impact, is a good first step. Now it's time to stand back and rethink them.

You may have one major Rule, or you may find you have more than one. If so, it's probably sensible to tackle them one at a time. Aim to change one Rule first, and then use what you learn to deal with the next, rather than trying to do a bit of everything and getting muddled. You could choose to start with the Rule that seems to be affecting your life most powerfully, or you could choose the one that might be easiest to change as your starting point.

When you have chosen a Rule to work on, ask yourself where it came from (you may already have some ideas about this from reading and thinking about Part 1). This doesn't mean dwelling on the past, but just understanding how the Rule developed and what's kept it going. Very often we made our Rules when we were very young, and often they were guidelines for what we needed to do to protect ourselves at the time. Later in life, we don't have the same external forces (such as parents and teachers), and our Rules are no longer helpful to us, but they've become so firmly ingrained that we carry on acting as if they're still useful. Understanding why we think as we do can be the first step to realising that we no longer need to obey the Rules. Chloe, for example, really needed to keep quiet and not stand up for herself, because she needed to protect herself from her stepfather's anger. As a young child she had very little choice, and the Rule *did* help keep her out of harm's way. But as we've seen, as an adult the Rule started to make her feel worse about herself and allowed other people to take advantage of her.

Here are some questions to help you to step back from your Rules, take a fresh look at them, and look for a more realistic and kinder perspective:

- In what ways is your Rule unreasonable? Does it actually fit the way the world works? Does it ask more of you than is possible for any normal human being?

- What are the benefits of obeying the Rule?

- What are the disadvantages?

- What alternative Rule would be more realistic and helpful? See if you can find something that will allow you more freedom of movement to be yourself, that encourages you to accept and appreciate yourself just as you are.

- What do you need to do to 'test-drive' your new Rule? How can you go about putting it into practice every day?

As you work through these questions, make sure you summarise what you are discovering in writing, either on paper or electronically. This will help you to remember what you have done, and build on it. It may not be easy to come up with a fairer and more realistic new Rule, and you may even be tempted to hang on to old Rules that have worked at least partially for you throughout your life. Trying to develop a new Rule may feel like being out at sea without a lifejacket! You may find it difficult to get the exact words right or feel that what you've written doesn't exactly get to the point. Don't worry too much about this – this is your first draft, so just give it your best shot. You can always come back and change it as you get more familiar with the territory. Putting it into practice and seeing what happens will help you with this.

STEP 3: Putting the New Rule into Practice

This is the really important bit! If we make a new Rule, but still behave as if the old Rule is true, then the new one has absolutely no-chance of growing and flourishing. Difficult as it may be, you need to begin behaving as if the new Rule is true, even if this feels strange or awkward or even scary. It's the only way to make the new Rule part of your life. So, spend some time considering: How would someone who genuinely believed my new Rule behave? You may find it helpful not just to think about this, but to imagine vividly what such a person might do, what their thoughts would be, how they would feel.

In the end, Chloe decided that she really had to change her old Rule. She realised that it was making her unhappy and making her self-esteem worse. She thought hard about what would make a good new Rule and came up with: 'I have the right to stick up for myself and be as fair to myself as I would be to anyone else.' She worked very hard to put this Rule into practice, and although it was difficult she started to see that people did respond to it. Meg, for instance, realised that she'd behaved badly, and agreed to take the coat to the cleaners.

Remember: direct experience is the best teacher. The more you experiment with behaving as if the new Rule is true, the more you'll be able to see if it works better for you, and fine-tune it if you need to. And the easier it will be to believe it.

12

Creating a New Bottom Line

As we've seen, your Bottom Line (your sense that you are worthless, useless, unlovable or whatever) drives your Rules for Living, and fuels your anxious predictions and self-critical thinking. And all of these things keep you stuck in low self-esteem. This means that everything you have already done to rethink your anxious and self-critical thoughts and your Rules, and to experiment with doing things differently, makes a solid foundation for creating a new, kinder view of yourself.

We hope that you'll already have started to make changes in how you think and act. If so, you may have noticed that the Bottom Line doesn't seem quite so overwhelmingly true as it once did. Now is the time to tackle it directly. Even if you have not noticed any change yet, don't worry. Some people only start to change how they feel when they get to grips with the Bottom Line.

There are four key steps to creating a new Bottom Line:

1. Identifying your old Bottom Line (awareness).

2. Undermining your old Bottom Line: examining the evidence (rethinking).

3. Identifying your new Bottom Line (rethinking).

4. Strengthening your new Bottom Line (rethinking and experiments).

STEP 1: Identifying Your Old Bottom Line

At the beginning of Part 2 we asked a number of questions to help you to identify your Bottom Line and where it came from, and hopefully the following sections have helped you to see how it is operating in your life. It may be worth looking at that old Bottom Line again. You could use the information you've gained from the previous sections to help.

*   *Look at your anxious predictions*. If they had come true, what would that have meant? What would it have said about you as a person?

*   *Look at your self-critical thoughts*. Are there words and phrases that come up again and again? Are the words you use to criticise yourself the same as words other people used when you were small? The words you use to criticise yourself can also be pretty much a mirror image of your Bottom Line.

- *Look at your Rules*. Think what would happen if you broke them. For example, if you think you should always keep busy, what would it mean if you didn't? Perhaps it might be 'I'm a lazy good-for-nothing.' Could this be your Bottom Line? Think about the consequences for how you feel about yourself if you don't live up to your Rules.

- *Think again about your early history*. What happened in your life to make you feel badly about yourself? How did other people treat you? Who comes into your mind when you remember feeling bad? Whose voice do you hear? What kind of things did they say? What messages were you given about yourself?

STEP 2: Undermining Your Old Bottom Line: Examining the Evidence

Undermining the old Bottom Line means working out exactly what evidence you think backs it up. And then you need to find out if there are other ways to understand that 'evidence'. For example, we know that Jen thinks that she is unlovable and that no one wants to have anything to do with her. Her daughter has started at a new school, and she dreads having to go and pick her up. She thinks about the group of mothers that she sees at the school gate. They all talk to each other, and then they go off and have coffee with each other. They never talk to her or invite her along. This does indeed look like evidence that she is unwanted. But in fact, a friend who does seem to like her said, 'Why do you always glare at the other mums? You look really terrifying!' So, Jen came to understand that the other mothers didn't talk to her because (without meaning to) she was putting them off, rather than smiling and saying hello. And she realised that she had been doing this because she had assumed – made an anxious prediction – that they wouldn't like her. So, what seemed like good evidence really wasn't true after all.

Every time that you collect evidence that *appears* to support the old Bottom Line, ask yourself: 'Is there another way to explain what's happening, other than assuming it's because of me and what I am?'

There are a number of other questions you can ask when you examine the evidence:

- *Is it something to do with the other people, not me?* In the example above it could be that those mothers have known each other for years, stick together, and don't talk to *anyone* except each other? Can you explain what people do without putting yourself in the picture? Of course, sometimes it may be something to do with you – like Jen's shyness putting people off. But notice the difference here between what she thinks ('It's because I'm unlovable') and what is actually more likely ('It's because of something I'm doing'). In the first case, you're stuck with it – it's who you are. In the second case, you have the possibility of doing something different.

- *Is it fair to judge yourself on the basis of your short-comings?* Having some faults and weaknesses doesn't mean that your Bottom Line is true. It means that you are just like every other human being on the face of the earth – less than perfect.

- *Is it helpful to compare yourself to other people?* It is tempting to compare yourself to other people and say, 'Well, they're better-looking/richer/cleverer/more successful than me, so it proves I'm no good.' In fact, unless you're Superman or Wonder Woman there will *always* be someone who's better than you at something. Your worth *does not depend* on where you stand in some invented ranking of status or characteristics.

So, when you think that you've found evidence to support your old Bottom Line, make absolutely sure that there's no other explanation. Remember the court of law – you have to convince the jury that there is no other way of seeing things before they will convict you!

STEP 3: Identifying Your New Bottom Line

Once you're clear about your Bottom Line, it's time to formulate a new, kinder and more accepting idea of yourself – a new 'I am . . .' It'll be much easier to undermine and weaken your old Bottom Line if you have some idea of where you are heading. Otherwise it might be a bit like moving out of one house when you don't have a new one to move into. For instance, if your old Bottom Line was 'I am useless', try to find a form of words that would make it possible for you to move in the new Bottom Line's direction. Remember what we said about healthy self-esteem: it's about having a fair and balanced view of yourself which recognises that, like everyone else, you have weaknesses and flaws, alongside an equal recognition of your strengths and good points and, at heart, a sense that it's OK to be you. So, aim to come up with something realistic such as 'I am quite nice and there are at least some things about me that are good,' rather than, 'I am the most wonderful person who ever walked the earth.' Make sure that your new Bottom Line is fair and balanced, and not so over the top that you'll never believe it.

One way of finding a new Bottom Line is to ask yourself the following question:

'If I were not .... [the old Bottom Line], how would I like to be?'

Or you could call to mind someone who knows you well and whose opinion you trust. What might they say about you that would be fairer and more reasonable than your own view?

Whichever option you choose, write down what you have come up with. 'I am . . .' – what? Then, to get a feel for your new 'I am . . .', go back to a recent situation where your old Bottom Line was active, and imagine as vividly as you can how things would have played out if this new Bottom Line had been in place. Do you have the feeling that things would gone better for you and you would have felt better about yourself? Don't worry if it does not feel very convincing to you right now – it's brand new and you will need time and practice to start believing it strongly.

The trick now is to make your new Bottom Line into a kind of emotional bank account. If you think of it like this, then you can see that your old Bottom Line bank account has been accumulating interest for a long time and has a vast amount in it to back it up. At the moment your new account probably doesn't have much – but every time you notice anything good about yourself, in the ways we described earlier, you can 'deposit' it in the new account and watch it grow.

Note as well that your new Bottom Line doesn't pretend that you don't have flaws and weaknesses – of course you do. Why should you be the only person ever who was perfect? But the flaws do not sum you up and are not a sound basis for assessing your worth.

STEP 4: Strengthening Your New Bottom Line

The next step is to find ways of strengthening your new Bottom Line, and making it feel more convincing. You are OK. You are likeable. You are a reasonable person. What evidence do you have that this is true? Start to collect as much as you can – the tasks that you have carried out earlier should help to start your collection.

To be fair, you should examine the evidence in favour of your new Bottom Line carefully as well. But remember: you are much better at ignoring evidence for the good than you are at ignoring evidence for the bad. So, be fair to yourself. You are working to help a new habit of seeing good things about yourself sink in and become a routine part of how you operate. If this is difficult (it may well be, to start with) see if there's anyone else you could ask who would be able to help you put things in perspective. You could even get a low self-esteem buddy!

And don't forget to experiment, especially with acting as if your new Bottom Line was true (even if you do not fully believe it) and observing the outcome. Once again, be sure to keep a written record. Recording your discoveries will help you to remember them and give you something to look back on at those moments when you are feeling stressed or low, or your self-esteem has taken a knock. If you behave as if your new Bottom Line is true, it'll get stronger and stronger, and will come to feel more and more natural to you.

13

Planning for the Future

We hope that by now you've learned a lot about your low self-esteem and how to create a new, kinder and more accepting view of yourself and that you have begun to act on it in your everyday life. However, it is possible that, unless you continue to put what you have learned into practice on a regular basis, your new insights and ways of treating yourself with kindness will weaken and decay. As we have said before, old habits die hard. And new ones take time and practice to settle in. Particularly at times when you are stressed or pressured, or when you are feeling low or unwell or tired or under par, you may find that your Old Bottom Line will surface again.

This is not something you need worry about. What's important is not that you have occasional setbacks (these are a normal part of the journey towards healthy self-esteem), but rather what happens next. Up until now, your old Bottom Line has seemed powerful and convincing to you, and your Rules a necessary way of coping with it. The vicious circle of negative predictions and self-critical thinking has therefore had a strong pull, keeping you stuck in low self-esteem. But now you can see things differently. Now you understand how low self-esteem works, and you have a range of skills that you can call on if the old Bottom Line pops up again. So long as you can spot the signals that tell you that your sense of self-esteem is beginning to wobble, you are in a good position to do something about it.

Now is the time to think ahead and plan how to continue your journey appreciating yourself just as you are. Start by looking back over everything you have done, and summing up in writing what you have learned. This is your basis for deciding how best to take things forward. Here are some guiding questions to help you. Don't rush this – it may even be helpful to come back to the questions and fine-tune your answers several times. Take time to think your answers through, until you feel you have a good summary of how things have been for you, what you have learned and how you will use it in future.

How did my low self-esteem develop? What experiences led you to think badly of yourself?

What kept it going? It would be helpful here to identify your Rules for Living, your anxious predictions and precautions, and your self-critical thoughts – they have all kept your low self-esteem going. Use the flowchart on p.25 if you find it helpful.

What have I learned from this book? Make a note of new ideas that you've found helpful – for example, 'My beliefs about myself are opinions, not facts.' Include techniques that have been useful, such as reviewing the evidence properly, or checking things out in real life.

What were my most important unhelpful thoughts, Rules and beliefs? What alternatives did I find to them? Go back to the ones that seemed to cause you most distress. Sum up the alternatives that you have discovered. You could do this by creating your own chart (paper or electronic), a page with a vertical line drawn down the middle. Then write your old ideas on the left and your alternatives on the right, so you can see clearly where you started and where you have travelled to already.

How can I build on what I have learned? This is your opportunity to think ahead and make an action plan. How will you carry on the good work? Are there parts of the book that you need to go back to and work on in more depth? What goals would you like to achieve? Do you want to read more, or get help from other people? Remember that goals should be: Specific – say exactly what you're going to do and when you're going to do it; Realistic – don't set yourself targets that you won't be able to meet; and Measurable – so you'll know when you've got there.

What might lead to a setback for me? What kind of situations might make you vulnerable to setbacks? For example, spending time with people from the past who are very critical. What signals (thoughts, feelings, sensations in your body, action patterns) might tell you all is not well and that you need to do something to deal with what is happening?

If I do have a setback, what will I do about it? It's very common to have setbacks and ups and downs when getting over problems that have lasted a long time. It's normal, not the end of the world, so there's no need to panic. Make an action plan for how you'll use your new knowledge and skills to cope with setbacks. And remember that, if you do have a setback and you observe closely what is happening, although it will be unpleasant, it's a great opportunity to find out more about how your low self-esteem operates, because there it will be, doing what it does in front of your very eyes. So, although naturally you would rather not have setbacks, you can learn from them and use them as a basis for making your action plan even stronger in future.

A Final Word of Encouragement

This book provides information about low self-esteem, how it develops, what keeps it going and how you can create a new, more accepting, kind and respectful view of yourself – a sense that it's OK to be you, just as you are. Low self-esteem often develops when we're young and vulnerable and has a very powerful hold over our minds. So, changing it is sometimes painful and often slow. Remember that a journey of a thousand miles begins with one small step, and take your first step. Hard though it may be to believe you can change, you can. We wish you the very best of luck.

Other Things that Might Help

If this book has helped you but you would like to take it further, or if you feel that you need a different kind of approach, don't worry. Self-help is not for everyone, and there are many other resources available.

Make an appointment to see your family doctor and ask about alternatives. You may benefit from help with applying the ideas and strategies in this book from a psychologist or health worker, since research tells us that self-help works better if you have someone supporting you. Or you may benefit from more formal therapy.

If you would like to find out more about the approach we have taken here, we recommend the following self-help books:

Overcoming Low Self-Esteem by Melanie Fennell, published by Robinson (2016).

A paperback-length book that explains these ideas in more depth.

Overcoming Low Self-Esteem Self-Help Course by Melanie Fennell, also published by Robinson (2006). This is a three-part programme that goes into much more detail, with many examples and opportunities for you to make notes and keep records for yourself.

Overcoming Depression by Paul Gilbert,
published by Robinson (2009).

Overcoming Anxiety by Helen Kennerley,
published by Robinson (2014).

Overcoming Perfectionism by Roz Shafran,
Sarah Egan and Tracey Wade,
published by Robinson (2018).

If you like the cognitive behavioural approach we have used, it might be worth finding a qualified cognitive behavioural therapist. The following organisation will help you to find a therapist near you:

British Association for Behavioural and Cognitive Psychotherapies
Tel: 0330 320 0851 Email: babcp@babcp.com
website: www.babcp.com

Blank Worksheets

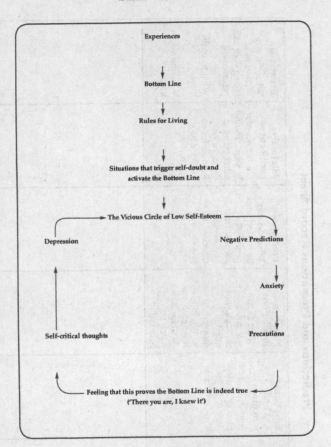

Experiences

↓

Bottom Line

↓

Rules for Living

↓

Situations that trigger self-doubt and
activate the Bottom Line

↓

The Vicious Circle of Low Self-Esteem

Depression   Negative Predictions

↓

Anxiety

↓

Self-critical thoughts   Precautions

Feeling that this proves the Bottom Line is indeed true
('There you are, I knew it')

Predictions and Precautions Record Sheet

Date/time	Situation What were you doing when you began to feel anxious?	Emotions and body sensations (e.g. anxious, panicky, tense) Rate 0–10 for how bad it was	Negative predictions What exactly was going through your mind (e.g. thoughts in words, images)? Rate each one 0–10 for how much you believed it	Precautions What did you do to stop your predictions from coming true (e.g. avoid the situation, take precautions)?	Alternative perspectives Use the questions in Step 2 to find other views of the situation. Rate each one 0–10 for how much you believe it	Experiment What did you do instead of taking your usual precautions? What were the results? What did you learn?

Dealing with Self-critical Thoughts

Date/time	Situation	Emotions and body sensations	Self-critical thoughts	Alternative perspectives	Outcome
	What were you doing when you began to feel bad about yourself?	(e.g. sad, angry, tense, stomach churning). Rate how bad each was 0–10	What exactly was going through your mind when you started to feel bad about yourself? How far did you believe each thought? (Rate 0–10)	Use the questions in Step 2 to find other ways of seeing yourself. Rate belief in each (0–10)	1. How do you feel after coming up with alternatives (0–10)? 2. How far do you now believe the critical thoughts (0–10)? 3. What can you do now (action plan, experiment)?

OVERCOMING
Low
Self-Esteem

2nd Edition

A self-help guide
using cognitive
behavioural techniques

an
OVERCOMING
publication

MELANIE FENNELL

READING
WELL

0

Overcoming Low Self-Esteem, 2nd Edition

'A thoroughly enjoyable read, and [I] would recommend trainee therapists read it also, as it will increase your understanding of the treatment of low self-esteem'

BABCP Magazine

Low self-esteem can make life difficult in all sorts of ways. It can make you anxious and unhappy, tormented by doubts and self-critical thoughts. It can get in the way of feeling at ease with other people and stop you from leading the life you want to lead. It makes it hard to value and appreciate yourself in the same way you would another person you care about.

Melanie Fennell's acclaimed and bestselling self-help guide will help you to understand your low self-esteem and break out of the vicious circle of distress, unhelpful behaviour and self-destructive thinking. Using practical techniques from Cognitive Behavioural Therapy (CBT), this book will help you learn the art of self-acceptance and so transform your sense of yourself for the better.

Specifically, you will learn:

- How low self-esteem develops and what keeps it going

- How to question your negative thoughts and the attitudes that underlie them

- How to identify your strengths and good qualities for a more balanced, kindly view of yourself

Overcoming self-help guides use clinically proven techniques to treat long-standing and disabling conditions, both psychological and physical. Many guides in the Overcoming series are recommended under the Reading Well Books on Prescription scheme.